TODD CETI
International Business Leader,

The
3 Pillars
of
Elite Results

*The Mindset, Leadership and Culture You Need
to Succeed in Business, Sports and Life*

PRAISE FOR
THE 3 PILLARS OF ELITE RESULTS

"*The 3 Pillars of Elite Results* should be required reading for every business owner and entrepreneur. The principles taught in this book I applied daily when I was a Navy SEAL and SEAL Instructor. I also apply these same principles now as a father and business owner. If you want to succeed at anything, it all starts with Todd Cetnar's strategies around mindset, leadership and culture."

Sean Haggerty
Former Navy SEAL & Navy SEAL Instructor
CEO, Protector Brewery
San Diego's First and Only Organic Brewery

"As a former Major League Baseball pitcher, you learn that setting your intention and moving from preference to principle make all the difference in managing the demands and pressure you experience at the highest levels of competition. In this book, Todd shares a lot of what I used in my career to perform at the highest level."

Jonah Bayliss, MPM
Former MLB Pitcher

"Once you start reading this book, you won't stop. WOW! I nearly underlined the entire book."

Eric Davis
Middle School Principal

"The principles set forth in this book and Todd's philosophies are life altering. This is a MUST read for any person wanting to perform at their ultimate best. I have begun to recommend this book to all of my patients. The 3 Pillars of Elite Results is revolutionary; not only is it practical and motivational, but the strategies are amazing!"

Dr. Salya Namazi
Clinical Psychologist

"A must-read for anyone who wants to accelerate their results."

Tommy Dyer
Vice President, Siemens

"Todd was so impactful as our annual conference keynote speaker that we asked him to come back for a second year in a row. This book and the skills contained within it, sustained the motivation and professional development in our staff like I have never seen in my 30+ years working in corporate America. This book really helps you move your results from temporary to legendary."

Tony Love
Lavoie Realty

Todd Cetnar, MPM
Cetnar Consulting Group, LLC

The 3 Pillars of Elite Results
The Mindset, Leadership and Culture You Need to
Succeed in Business, Sports and Life

©2021 by Todd Cetnar, MPM

Printed in the United States of America
Edited by: Mary Lou Reynolds

*This book is dedicated
to my wife and daughter.*

*In loving memory
of our two fur children Bella and Jersey.*

INTRODUCTION

It was only a matter of time.

When you're going through a global pandemic, the odds are never in your favor. Then again, for Michael Stoneridge, the odds have never been in his favor.

Having grown up in Boser Springs, New York, Michael had overcome odds his entire life. The small-town kid had gone on to be a successful collegiate athlete; married Amelia, the woman of his dreams; and ascended to the top of the corporate ladder in his 18 years with Bella Medical Company to become the Vice President of Sales, managing a team of 2,500 people.

Now 40 years old, he had been with the company for nearly two decades and with his Amelia for almost 12 years. Always an ambitious go-getter and a goal-oriented, focused and driven achiever, Michael was underperforming. Underperforming at the office and at home.

After being tagged with contact tracing, he was sent home from the office to quarantine for three days, with a clear message from his boss, Robert Coachman, the CEO of Bella Medical Company:

"Either you change and grow, or it's time we make a change and you go," was Robert's message.

"Take this quarantine and do some soul-searching. You are not the same guy we promoted. Something's off; you've become a transactional leader and we're a transformational company," Robert said. "When you come back, have a plan of attack to become the best version of yourself and to level up your performance or don't come back at all."

As Michael walked to his car to drive home and start his quarantine, he felt like he had taken a one-two to the gut. The one was the quarantine. The two was the harsh yet honest feedback from his boss.

CHAPTER 1
Grow or Go

"Amelia, I'm on my way home. I got hit with contact tracing and need to quarantine for three days," Michael said to his wife while driving the 30 minutes home from the office. "I also met with Robert and he basically told me that it was time to either grow or go."

"I'm sorry to hear that, Michael, and I'm not surprised," Amelia said. "You aren't the most diligent at wearing a mask, washing your hands or watching your distance. You also haven't been very motivated since this pandemic, if I were to be honest. I've been reminding you, that in this 'new world' you either evolve or become extinct.

"I've got a huge week at school and Rhys [pronounced Reese] has a big tournament this week. I don't want us to risk catching what you got; please go to the pool house and do your quarantine out there. I will see you when I get home. Drive safe."

As Michael drove home, he felt a mix of emotions. Not only was he at a pivotal crossroads in his business career, his life at home wasn't the strongest either.

He hadn't been to one of his daughter's basketball games since she was eight years old. Now 10 and in 4th grade, Rhys acted as if she were in her 4th year of college. He felt like she was 10 going on 20 and he had missed much of her developmental years, traveling once a week for the last two decades for work.

He actually couldn't remember the last time he was in one place for three days, let alone being banished to the pool house, a one-room casita by the pool in their backyard that was usually reserved for friends or family who came into town. And come to think of it, Michael couldn't remember the last time someone stayed the night there.

Frustrated, a bit angry and unsure of how the next three days would unfold, Michael pulled into the garage, walked into the backyard, and was greeted by his 12-year-old boxer named Jersey. He and the family called her "Jerz," pronounced as if the "ey" had been dropped.

Getting kisses and scratching Jerz's spotted belly was about the only routine Michael had in his life at the moment. He and his dog walked to the pool house for what looked and felt like more of a 3-day jail sentence than a vacation.

CHAPTER 2
The Pool House

Upon entering the pool house, Michael noticed how long it had been since he had stepped foot inside.

The one-room casita had a small bathroom and a small kitchen area, a far cry from the beautiful house Michael and Amelia had built when he got his promotion.

The main living area had a travertine tile floor with a flagstone fireplace and a flat-screen TV with Rhys's video games hooked up to it.

Michael reflected on the days when Rhys was younger and they used to compete in Mario Kart and other games she loved as a kid.

He couldn't remember the last time they had played, as he was always too busy working during the week or watching golf and football on TV during the weekends.

On a wall across from the pull-out couch, which would be his bed for the next three days, was this sign: "The Attitude You Take Is A Decision You Make." Michael chuckled as he looked at the sign and thought to himself, *Well... I needed to see that.*

In the kitchen were all Whirlpool stainless steel appliances that looked brand new. They probably hadn't been used in years.

Michael went to the fridge and, as he expected, Amelia had it stocked with water, soda and beer. Since it was only 9:30am, although the thought that it was 5 o'clock somewhere entered his mind, he settled on a cup of coffee, sat on the couch and opened up his laptop to start his workday.

As he attempted to connect to the pool house WIFI, Jerz walked in, hopped up on the couch next to him and put her head on his lap.

Pushing her head away so he could check his email, he looked back up at the sign on the wall: *The Attitude You Take Is A Decision You Make*.

He then reached over, scratched the dent between Jerz's eyes and thought, *At least Jerz loves me*.

CHAPTER 3
Inbox Overwhelm

Once his laptop was up and running, and after searching for 20 minutes to find the password to connect to the guesthouse WIFI, Michael opened up his inbox as he normally did to start his day.

And 235 new emails sat waiting for him with another 400+ opened and taking up space in his inbox. Feeling like a human network router, Michael quickly clicked over to a new browser window and for the next 15 minutes welcomed the distraction of Instagram.

Finally, the internal voice of reason kicked in. After looking at an "Improve Your Chipping" golf video, highlights of Steph Curry's game last night and mixed martial arts replays, he said to himself, "Dude, what are you doing? Get to work!"

Now with more than 260 new emails, Michael took a sip of coffee and went to work.

This was a typical day for Michael – working from his inbox, repeatedly distracting himself with social media or checking ESPN updates. At 4pm and with 90+ new emails still in his inbox, he heard a knock on the pool house glass door slider.

CHAPTER 4
Welcome Home

Amelia opened the slider door and with her mask on, she stayed in the entrance to the pool house.

"How are you feeling?" she asked.

"I'm good. Just workin'. Trying to get this inbox cleared."

"What else is new?" she said in a rhetorical manner. "Look, Michael. I've been wanting to talk to you, but you're always so busy with work and with your laptop that it's just been easier for me to put this off.   It's never easy having hard conversations, you know."

In my mind I was thinking that I could relate. I'd been putting off hard conversations with my team of 2,500 at Bella Medical for months since the pandemic hit. We had furloughed more than 500 employees and everyone was on edge about who was next. I had intentionally avoided my team because people wanted to know what was coming and I didn't have any answers for them. Also, I never felt comfortable with the uncomfortableness of delivering bad news.

"I've been thinking. I'm not happy, Michael. I feel like I have a roommate more than a husband. You never ask me about how my days have gone or what's happening with Rhys; you just tell me about all you have going on at work and where you're headed next," Amelia said. "I hope while you are home for these three days you are able to do some reflection about what's important to you, and not only where Bella Medical is going but where WE are going. I'm heading out to the store now. Text me if you think you need anything."

Although I was pretty content with water, coffee and beer, I figured I'd have Amelia get some pre-made food for the week so I could hunker down in the pool house.

As she walked away, headed to the store to once again do more for me, I couldn't help but agree with what she said about "where WE are going." I hated to admit it, but I hadn't been the best husband or father lately. And as I looked at the photos on the wall of Amelia, Rhys and me at the beach, I realized I was far from the physical shape I was in just three years ago when we went to Amelia Island, Florida, for family vacation.

We had convinced Rhys that it was "Mommy's Island" for a while. But I guess, just like kids with Santa Claus, all good things come to an end, and for the first time I wondered if my marriage and my job could be next.

CHAPTER 5
The Gut Check

As I sat in the pool house, I pondered my future.

Three days in quarantine.

Underperforming in my job.

Underperforming as a husband and a father.

Underperforming in my fitness.

It was a gut check for sure. I'd always had confidence in myself, but I'd been rocked. Whether it was the changing times at work or in the world, or my obsession with chasing success, I WAS underperforming and letting down those who mean the most to me.

My father, who was a successful coach, had always told me that he had only one rule on his teams: "Don't let your teammates down." I was doing exactly that. I was letting down my team at work and my team at home.

People were leaving to go to our competitors, and I had lost the connection I once had with my employees.

I began my career as an intelligent business leader who wanted to simply serve others and make a difference by educating, empowering and energizing people. However, somewhere along the line I ended up trying to be viewed as the smartest and most powerful person. I even told myself that it was working and rationalized my behavior; I was really just telling myself lies.

I was underperforming and was scared of losing my job and losing my family. I just didn't know what to do so I kept on doing what I knew, which was working, traveling and keeping myself busy.

As much as I hated to admit it, I had been confusing busyness with business and now that I was alone in quarantine for three days, it was like three years of reflection hitting me at once.

I felt like I was on a train and somehow it was headed in the wrong direction... I just didn't know how to get off or get it turned around.

At least I had Jerz.

CHAPTER 6
"Come Here, Jersey"

"Jersey, Jersey. Come here, girl."

I had never heard that voice before.

Jerz shot up from the couch, her nails digging into my leg as she sprang from a deep sleep on the couch and ran out the door as only a 60-lb boxer can do.

"Good girl. Ready to go for a walk? Want to go for a walk?" I heard the man say as he was petting my dog and I walked towards him.

"Hello," I said. "Can I help you?"

"Hi. I'm Rick from Rick's Dog Walking Service. Are you Mr. Stoneridge?" the man asked.

"Yes. Nice to meet you. Are you here to walk Jerz?"

"Yes, Mr. Stoneridge. Been coming four days a week for the last four years. Gotta keep this boxer on the move. Motion is lotion when you get to her age. Heck, motion is lotion for all of us. We don't stop moving when we get old; we get old when we stop moving. It's nice to finally meet you. Amelia has told me all about you."

"Well, it's nice to meet you too, Rick, I didn't realize that we had a dog walking service for Jerz," I said with a smile, thinking to myself, *How did I not know that we have had a dog walking service for the last four years?*

"Yeah, crazy to think that I've been coming to your house to walk your dog four days a week for four years and this is the first time we've met," Rick commented. "What's the occasion?"

"Got hit with a contact tracing at work so I'm home for the next three days," I replied a bit dejectedly.

"Been there, done that, Mr. Stoneridge. It's most likely only a matter of time for us all before we catch it or get hit with a contact tracing," Rick said. "Good news for me is that I've now got the antibodies and also got a vaccine shot since I walk a lot of elderly people's dogs and my wife's a nurse. That being the case, you want to mask up and go on this walk with Jersey and me? Always fun for our four-legged fur babies to show off to their parents."

"I've got some work to do, Rick," I said. "But heck, I've got nowhere to be for the next three days, so why not? Let me put my shoes on and let's go. I can't remember the last time I walked Jerz and who knows how many more walks she has in her?"

I put my shoes on and we headed out the gate towards the canal by the house. It felt good to get out and move. I used to live an active life but had become pretty sedentary in the last few years, so any exercise I could get would be a step in the right direction, literally.

CHAPTER 7
One Day, Three Times

"You know, Mr. Stoneridge, a strategy I used to help keep my mind right when I was in quarantine was to look at it one day three times, versus being in isolation for three days. I felt like it was easier for me to process it that way," Rick said as we walked Jerz on the canal. "I looked at it like dog walking. I don't walk 10 dogs in a day; I walk one dog 10 times. It helps me to stay present and give my best to each dog that day. Dogs are pretty good at reading a human's presence. It's like a sense they have better than we do as humans."

"One day three times. I like that," I responded. "I think that will help me. I have been a little overwhelmed with not being in the office or on the road for the next three days, I don't want to fall behind on my work. I haven't been home for a three-day period of time since I can remember."

"Well, Mr. Stoneridge, I think you'll find that mindset beneficial. It's something that I've found helps me to be where my feet are, to be present. And it's our presence that is our greatest gift to the world," Rick said. "I used to be someone who would count the days, meaning count the days until the weekend. However, now I focus on making each day count. Attitude is a decision, you know."

"Funny you mentioned that, Rick. We have that slogan on a sign in our pool house," I remarked.

"No kidding? That is funny. Respectfully, I don't think of *attitude is a decision* as a slogan, Mr. Stoneridge," Rick replied. I see it as a mindset. It's a lifestyle, not an event. The attitude you take is a decision you make and it's unquestionably the most important decision you make on a daily basis, pandemic or no-demic. I also think mindset is our greatest skill set, especially amidst a pandemic when there's so much uncertainty and you have to be able to adapt and adjust day to day."

It felt like I was in the presence of a motivational speaker, not a dog walker. Rick had a unique perspective, one that I felt like I had lost over the years. I used to be more positive, more optimistic.

"Rick, I like where your head is at. I need some of this positivity right now."

"Mr. Stoneridge, it's my pleasure," Rick said as Jerz stopped to sniff a bush. "I look at our mindset a lot like a dog's sniffer. Jersey uses her sniffer to experience her world. It's like dogs use their nose as a gateway to the world. I think that's what we do as humans; we use our mindset as a gateway to the world. It's our mindset that dictates whether this pandemic is happening to us or for us. It's our mindset that allows us to make adversity our advantage. Our mindset determines if we are going to bring the juice. And as one of my friends, Matthew Simonds, says, 'If you're juiceful, you're useful and if you're juiceless, you're useless.'"

"Rick, you are bringing the juice today, that's for sure," I shared with my new friend and dog walking partner. "Keep feeding me this. I need more of this. I need a little checkup from the neck up."

"My pleasure, Mr. Stoneridge," Rick stated as we started walking again and Jerz engaged another bush. "I enjoy sharing what I have learned and look at it as being a lifter versus a leaner. For years I just went through the motions; I was GOING through life versus GROWING through life.

"Then one day I made a decision that I was going to be a fountain, not a drain – as I said, a lifter, not a leaner. A lifter lifts people up; a leaner leans on others to do the work or brings people down. I decided to become other people's spark, their lifter! I walked away from my 9–5 job and started Rick's Dog Walking Service, and it's been one of the best decisions of my life. But it had to become a mentality before it became a reality. Once I got my mind right, the results followed."

CHAPTER 8
Pillar #1 – Elite Mindset
Get Your Mind Right & Your Game Tight

Rick was on fire. You could feel his energy and his love for people, dogs and his profession. You couldn't help but feel uplifted in his presence.

"Rick, you are certainly a lifter, my friend. I needed this walk; I needed a little uplifting and you have done that. Thank you."

"My pleasure, Mr. Stoneridge," Rick replied. "If I may, I'd like to share some more about mindset if you're up for it? I've been working on building the eight skills of an elite mindset and would love to share with you what I've learned. I wish I had learned them earlier in life, but like a tree, the best time to plant a tree would have been 20 years ago because now it would be full grown. The second-best time to plant a tree is right now.

"I'm focused on being where my feet are, getting my mind right and my game tight. I'm focused on winning the day, not agonizing about the past or stressing about the future, just stacking quality days on top of quality days. It's a mindset that I love to share because I love what that mindset has done for me, my business and my family."

"Rick, I'm all ears," I said. "Keep bringing the juice. I'd love to hear about the eight skills of your elite mindset. I could sure use that checkup from the neck up, as I mentioned."

As we both chuckled and kept walking, I felt like this was exactly what I needed: a mindset mentor, if you would. I just never thought it would come from a dog walker!

CHAPTER 9
Elite Mindset Skill #1
Physiology

"Mr. Stoneridge, I am a firm believer that our physiology affects our psychology and our psychology affects our physiology," Rick said. "I also am a believer that we should move our way into feeling, rather than feel our way into moving. Most people wait until they feel like moving their body to move, and the problem is that the feeling often never comes until you get started. It's the start that stops most people. I like to start my day with movement and getting my physiology in check to help get my psychology in check."

"Rick, what I'm hearing you say is that I've got to get my body right before I can get my mind right?" I asked.

"Pretty much spot on, Mr. Stoneridge. It's not an exact science, but it's about as close to exact as you can be. You move your body and your mindset follows. It's a big reason why I love my job. I am no longer sitting behind a desk staring at a screen all day; I am moving for most of the day," Rick replied. "I realize that not everyone has the luxury of movement baked into their jobs, but it should be baked into their daily lives and daily routines. I often call it my 'sweat before screens routine' with those I coach on the side."

"Sweat before screens. I love that, Rick," I said. "Amelia works out every morning before she goes to school and she has energy for days. She always asks me to join her, but I've just not done it."

"Well, you've not done it *YET*, Mr. Stoneridge," Rick reminded me. "You can plan that habit today, or maybe after your quarantine. Movement changes moods, action changes attitudes, and motion creates emotion. If you want to change your psychology (mindset) and your life, start by changing your physiology."

CHAPTER 10
Elite Mindset Skill #2
Focus & Awareness

"The second skill I share with the clients I coach is having better present-moment focus and increased self-awareness," Rick continued. "Our focus determines our future, and awareness is the first step in all growth. What you are aware of you can alter; what you are unaware of will alter you."

"Rick, I have never worked with a coach before. Is this what you work on with your clients – mindset, physiology, focus and awareness?" I asked. "I didn't know these were skills that you could develop. I thought you either had them or you didn't."

"Mr. Stoneridge, you are right on, sir. These and the other skills I will share with you to develop an elite mindset are exactly that, skills. And we do drills to develop skills, a lot like Rhys does to work on her basketball game. I see her do drills to develop the skills she needs to be a good hooper.

"Developing an elite mindset follows a similar process. You do drills to develop skills, and I teach physiology and focus/awareness as the first two skills of the eight you want to develop to have an elite mindset so that you can get elite results."

"Rick, how do you train focus? I feel like I spend most of my time distracted and I have a hard time focusing on what I need to do."

"Well, there are a few drills I do with myself and my clients to develop the skill of focus. We do meditation, concentration grids and some others," Rick said. "To keep it simple today, let's just make the commitment to be where your feet are, to not count the days but make the days count, and to remember that today + today + today = our lives, and in a work setting our careers. I'd suggest with your current situation that you look at your quarantine as one day three times and always remember tomorrow."

CHAPTER 11
Remember Tomorrow

"What do you mean by remember tomorrow?" I asked as Jerz took a drink from the canal and panted as if she were having the time of her life showing off for her two best friends.

"Most people go through life with a mentality of compete or act as if this were your last day," Rick answered. "While I get what they are after, I think you get more benefit by using the remember tomorrow strategy. Tomorrow will be here... What you do today will affect tomorrow. If you are organized, efficient and effective today, that sets up tomorrow. If you live like there's no tomorrow and go party and get hammered, that affects tomorrow. If you get a good night's sleep, go to bed early and get up early, that affects tomorrow. If you watch Netflix and watch other people live their lives versus invest into yours, that affects tomorrow. I just try to make my decisions today, thinking *how will this affect me and those I love tomorrow?* It helps me make the best next decisions I can today."

"I like that, Rick. That's a different spin," I said.

"A different spin or a different mindset. I like to look at it as a different focus and mindset," Rick replied. "It's like shifting from proving others wrong versus proving yourself right. They both create energy for you; you just have to find what works for you and use it to your advantage. We're constantly playing mental games with ourselves, and the better you get at the games you play with yourself, the better your behavior becomes and the better the results you get."

CHAPTER 12
Elite Mindset Skill #3
Process over Outcome

"The third skill that helps facilitate an elite mindset is keeping the process over the outcome. It's learning to control what you can, and learning to quickly let go of what you can't," Rick said. "I like to think that there's no use worrying about the things you can control because if you can control them, why worry? There's also no use worrying about the things you can't control because if you can't control them, why worry?"

"That's elite, Rick," I replied. "Have you always thought this way?"

"No, Mr. Stoneridge. I started to think this way when I worked with a mental performance coach named Coach Rags. I have worked with him as my coach for years. All coaches need coaches. It's the one thing that every Olympic athlete has, regardless of sport, gender, country; they all have coaches," Rick said. "Coach Rags helped me to better understand process over outcome when he had me make a list of what I could control and what I couldn't control. Putting those two lists side by side was an eye-opener for me; it definitely increased my awareness. He asked me how much of my time I spent on items on the list I couldn't control, and it was about 80%. The point was that 80% of my time, energy and attention was going to what I couldn't control so it was wasted time, energy and attention. I was like the kid with the magnifying glass trying to light a piece of paper, but I kept moving the magnifying glass all over instead of keeping it steady and harnessing the power of the sun to ignite the paper."

"Rick, I had no idea you were walking our dog four days a week for the last four years and I had no idea that you were a coach, either," I commented.

"It's all good, Mr. Stoneridge," Rick stated. "I love what I get to do every day. I get to walk with four-legged friends and I get to coach people I love and care about. I didn't begin with this type of business model in mind, but you know what? The people whose dogs I walk, as they starting walking with me, I began to use that time as our coaching session. It's been really, really fun and I am so blessed to get to do what I love to do."

"How many clients do you have now, Rick?"

"One, sir. The one I'm with," Rick said with a smile. "It may sound cliché but it's how I like to do it and it's worked for me."

"Are all of your clients the same? Like, do you have a specialty?"

"I'd like to think my specialty is people," Rick replied. "People and mindset. They go hand in hand because all people have a mindset; it's just not always the mindset they want or the mindset they need to get the results they want. I help them identify what they want, who they need to become and the mindset they need to get there."

"How do you manage all of the different personalities of the people you coach?" I asked. "I really struggle with managing all of the different personalities we have at Bella Medical."

"Mr. Stoneridge, I use a strategy I call 'flipping the mental switch.'"

CHAPTER 13
Flipping the Mental Switch

"The one thing about people is that they like other people who are like them. If you are going to connect and be able to serve a diverse group of people and personalities, you have to move from the Golden Rule to the Platinum Rule. And in order to do that you have to flip the mental switch."

"I've heard of the Golden Rule – treat others how you want to be treated – but what's the Platinum Rule?" I asked.

"The Platinum Rule is treating others how THEY want to be treated," Rick said. "What I like about the Platinum Rule is that it takes the focus off of you and puts it on others. Treat them how THEY want to be treated, now how you want to be treated.

"In order to do that, you have to be present and in order to be present, I like to flip the mental switch. Flipping the switch is a mindset strategy I use by snapping my fingers when I need to 'flip the mental switch.' It's like a trigger or anchor for me to be where my feet are and to dial into that moment, that person, their needs. I snap and it's like a light switch; it brings my energy on and gets me present. One of my golfer clients flips the switch on before every shot and off after every shot. It's been great for his game and great for my life."

After thinking about this, I responded, "Rick, I love that. I get pulled in so many directions during the day that if I had a trigger like 'flipping the mental switch' to get me back to the present I think I'd be more efficient."

"Mr. Stoneridge, I think you will find that 'flipping the mental switch' will make you more efficient and more effective. A part of my process is to also intentionally be efficient with things and tasks and effective with people. A lot of times, the corporate executive clients I have mix those up. They try to be effective with tasks and things, and efficient with people. When you reverse the two, it becomes a hindrance to your connection and relationship development with people."

Efficient versus effective... I was mixing those up for sure. I had never thought about it that way but could totally relate to the concept. That is one strategy I am going to deploy when I get back to the office and back into my house.

CHAPTER 14
Elite Mindset Skill #4
Discipline & Self-Mastery

As we turned around at the halfway point of our walk and headed back to the house, I was truly enjoying my time with Rick. He was living his mission. He was educating, empowering and energizing me on this walk and talk.

"Mr. Stoneridge, the fourth skill of an elite mindset is the skill of discipline and self-mastery," Rick said. "Unfortunately, *discipline* is a word that has been hijacked by society to have a negative connotation, like if your children misbehave, they get disciplined. In reality, discipline keeps you out of trouble, discipline keeps you productive, discipline keeps you living your best life. It's the lack of discipline that gets you in trouble."

"That makes sense, Rick," I agreed. "I've not been the most disciplined in the last few years with my physiology, my focus and my processes, and it's catching up to me. My results at work and in my house are not what I want them to be."

"Mr. Stoneridge, I completely understand," Rick replied. "The decision to grow or to stay the same is in your hands. It's up to you to decide which you will do. The time is now, the place is here. No sense in focusing on the *would have, should have*, or *could have.*

"Focus on your next best decision, and focus on starting your journey down the path of self-mastery. It's decisions in times like this that determine our destiny, similar to the decision that a guy named Easy Eddie was faced with years ago in the windy city of Chicago."

CHAPTER 15
Decisions Determine Destiny

"Many years ago, Al Capone virtually owned Chicago. Capone wasn't famous for anything heroic. He was notorious for enmeshing the Windy City in everything from bootlegged booze and prostitution, to murder," Rick said as he started to tell the story. "Capone had a lawyer nicknamed 'Easy Eddie.' He was Capone's lawyer for a good reason: Eddie was very good! In fact, Eddie's skill at legal maneuvering kept Big Al out of jail for a long time.

"To show his appreciation, Capone paid him very well. Not only was the money big, but Eddie got special dividends. For instance, he and his family occupied a fenced-in mansion with live-in help and all of the conveniences of the day. The estate was so large that it filled an entire Chicago city block.

"Eddie lived the high life of the Chicago mob and gave little consideration to the atrocity that went on around him. He did have one soft spot, however: a son that he loved dearly. Eddie saw to it that his young son had clothes, cars and a good education. Nothing was withheld. Price was no object.

"Despite his involvement with organized crime, Eddie even tried to teach him right from wrong.

Eddie wanted his son to be a better man than he was. He wanted his son to have a more honorable life than he did.

"Yet, with all his wealth and influence, there were two things he couldn't give his son; he couldn't pass on a good name or a good example. One day, Easy Eddie reached a difficult decision. Easy Eddie wanted to rectify the wrongs he had done... He wanted to start walking a path of self-mastery and start doing things right, to undo the wrong he had been a part of so that he could provide a better model for others. He knew an important leadership lesson: People, especially young people like his son or your daughter Rhys, need a model to see more than a motto to say. They need to see someone walk the walk and not just talk the talk.

"He decided he would go to the authorities and tell the truth about Al 'Scarface' Capone, clean up his tarnished name, and offer his son some semblance of integrity. To do this, he would have to testify against The Mob, and he knew that the cost would be great. He testified anyway.

"Within the year, Easy Eddie's life ended in a blaze of gunfire on a lonely, windy Chicago street. But in his eyes, he had given his son the greatest gift he had to offer, at the greatest price he could ever pay. Police removed from his pockets a rosary, a crucifix, a religious medallion, and a poem clipped from a magazine. This was the poem:

"The clock of life is wound but once and no man has the power to tell just when the hands will stop, at late or early hour. Now is the only time you own. Live, love, toil with a will. Place no faith in time. For the clock may soon be still."

"Wow, that's incredible," I said. "Talk about making a difficult decision!"

"Mr. Stoneridge, it gets better," Rick said as he continued into the story. "You know, World War II produced many heroes. One such man was Lieutenant Commander Butch O'Hare. He was a fighter pilot assigned to the aircraft carrier *Lexington* in the South Pacific.

"One day his entire squadron was sent on a mission. After he was airborne, he looked at his fuel gauge and realized that someone had forgotten to top off his fuel tank. He would not have enough fuel to complete his mission and get back to his ship. His flight leader told him to return to the carrier. Reluctantly, he dropped out of formation and headed back to the fleet.

"As he was returning to the mother ship, he saw something that turned his blood cold; a squadron of Japanese enemy aircraft was speeding its way toward the American fleet.

"The American fighters were gone on a sortie and the fleet was all but defenseless. He couldn't reach his squadron and bring them back in time to save the fleet. Nor could he warn the fleet of the approaching danger. There was only one thing to do. He must somehow divert the enemy from the fleet.

"Laying aside all thoughts of personal safety, he dove into the formation of Japanese planes. Wing-mounted 50 calibers blazed as he charged in, attacking one surprised enemy plane and then another. Butch wove in and out of the now-broken formation and fired at as many planes as possible until all his ammunition was finally spent.

"Undaunted, he continued the assault. He dove at the planes, trying to clip a wing or tail in hopes of damaging as many enemy planes as possible, rendering them unfit to fly. Finally, the exasperated Japanese squadron took off in another direction. Deeply relieved, Butch O'Hare and his tattered fighter limped back to the carrier.

"Upon arrival, he reported in and relayed the events surrounding his return. The film from the gun-camera mounted on his plane told the tale. It showed the extent of Butch's daring attempt to protect his fleet. He had, in fact, destroyed five enemy aircraft. This took place on February 20, 1942, and for that action Butch became the

Navy's first Ace of World War II, and the first Naval Aviator to win the Medal of Honor."

"I'd say that took an elite mindset," I remarked. "Wow! Thank God for our armed services men and women."

"Unfortunately, Mr. Stoneridge, a year later Butch was killed in aerial combat at the age of 29," Rick said with a somber tone. "However, his hometown would not allow the memory of this World War II hero to fade, and today O'Hare Airport in Chicago is named in tribute to the courage of this great warrior. So the next time you find yourself at O'Hare International, give some thought to visiting Butch's memorial displaying his statue and his Medal of Honor. It's located between Terminals 1 and 2, I think."

"I will do that, Rick," I responded. "I've flown through O'Hare a million times and never knew the story or have seen the memorial. I'm usually head down into my phone when walking."

"I understand, Mr. Stoneridge," Rick said. "You know the craziest part about those two stories... Butch O'Hare was Easy Eddie's son."

"Wow," I said. "Your decisions determine your destiny. If his dad had never come clean and set that example, who knows..."

"Crazy to think about it that way, sir," Rick replied. "What I love about that story is that one decision made during a difficult time literally impacted an event many years later. That's the power of decision. That's the power that walking the path of self-mastery has on others. People watch what you do and that influences how they live, the decisions they make and often, the trajectory of their lives. I don't think it's limited to your children either, as it was in the story of the O'Hares. I think this goes for all of us in positions of leadership.

"That's why the mindset of discipline and self-mastery are so important: They affect every decision we make, and decisions determine destiny."

CHAPTER 16
Elite Mindset Skill #5
Routines & Habits of Excellence

"The fifth skill I work to develop in those I coach is that of routines and habits of excellence. This is important in developing an elite mindset so we can get elite results," Rick continued. "I am a believer that the secrets of success are hidden in the routines of our daily lives. That our habits reflect our mission and goals in life. First we set our habits and routines. Our successes and failures are then created as a result of the influence that those routines and habits have on our daily behaviors."

"You know, Rick, Amelia is one of the most routine-oriented people I've ever met," I commented. "It was one of the first things that caught my eye about her years ago. She was so consistent, always energetic, always on time, always positive."

"Mr. Stoneridge, part of the process of becoming more consistent is creating the routines and habits you want intentionally to align with your goals. The bigger your goals, the tighter your process, routines and habits need to become."

"I've let my routines and habits slip," I admitted reluctantly. "The only routines and habits I seem to have are checking email, avoiding conflict, watching golf and football on weekends and right now, letting people like my boss and my wife down."

"Well, sir, the time is now and the place is here. You know where you will be for the next three days. Why don't you start by creating what your ideal day looks like and work to become a machine of routine for one day three times?" Rick suggested with a smile.

CHAPTER 17
Elite Mindset Skill #6
Time Management & Organization

"It has to start somewhere; it has to start sometime. What better place than here? What better time than now?" Rick asked.

"Sounds like the lyrics from 'Guerrilla Radio' by Rage Against the Machine?" I said, laughing.

"Matter of fact it is!" Rick was laughing even harder than I was. "I didn't know you were into the Rage. That's beautiful!

"All joking aside, Mr. Stoneridge, this quarantine that you are in is a great time to start building the routines and habits you want by scheduling your ideal day, being organized with your time, and being intentional with what you do and when.

"When I was in my quarantine, I had a routine where I blocked out my day and could then just go block by block, one block at a time like I go one dog at a time. It was actually a very productive three days, or should I say one day three times," Rick explained.

"That's a great idea, Rick. I'll try that. Hey, we're almost back to the house. Can you give me the other two skills of the elite mindset? And please, let me pay you for this impromptu coaching session."

"Ahh, you're too kind, Mr. Stoneridge," Rick replied. "No need to pay me for my time here today. You've been one of my best customers over the last four years. It's been great to finally meet you and put a face to a name.

"Now, the last two skills of an elite mindset."

CHAPTER 18
Elite Mindset Skill #7
Preparation & Mental Rehearsal

"I am a big believer that our separation is in preparation. Separation from our old self to our new self, from our previous best to our next best. Some would say from the competition, but WE ARE THE COMPETITION!!!" Rick said enthusiastically.

"Time is invested, not spent, sir. We don't spend time; we invest it, Mr. Stoneridge. Time invested into preparation saves time in execution. The time you take to prepare and map out your days will save you time in the execution of your days. It's like building a house with a blueprint versus from scratch. With a blueprint it'll be done better, faster and cost less in the end. There are two ways to do things: the right way and the wrong way. Again, if you don't have the time to invest into preparation up front, you won't have the time to redo the work that you don't do at an elite level. You will fall behind and become extinct."

"I agree 100%. I love that. I need to do that. I will plan out my days and then work my plan. Rick, that's genius," I said.

"Mr. Stoneridge, after preparation we need mental rehearsal, which is like intentional deja vu. It's a skill that Olympic athletes, Navy SEALs and actors use all the time. It's seeing the performance (or seeing the day) that you want in the movie theater of your mind before it happens. It's not Disney World or a magic pill; you still have to do the work and execute the plan, but mental rehearsal, aka visualization, is a big part of the preparation process that we often do as kids and then lose as adults."

Then Rick recalled a previous event: "You know, one day I was walking Jersey and on the way home Rhys was shooting hoops in the driveway. She kept counting down '3... 2... 1...' and shooting. She was in the championship game in her mind, making the game-winning shot. If she missed, she did it again. If she made it, she celebrated like she had just won the NCAA national championship. It was cute to watch. She was actually doing mental rehearsal and didn't even know she was practicing one of the skills of an elite mindset."

It was funny. I used to do a lot of mental rehearsal when I played college basketball. I always sat at my locker with a towel over my head and saw myself playing in the game that was about to start. I also would see every shot at the free throw line go into the hoop. That was similar to when I had putted my best in golf: I saw all the balls roll into the cup before I took my stroke.

"You know, Rick, I used to do a lot of mental rehearsal when I was playing hoops and in my golf game. I never thought about using it outside of sports," I explained.

"Mr. Stoneridge, mental rehearsal is a skill that we all do; we just don't do it with intention. I'd recommend that you invest a part of each day into visualizing or rehearsing how you want the rest of that day to go. Or, as part of your nightly routine, see in your mind's eye how you want tomorrow to go. It won't go exactly as planned, but it will help you be more efficient, effective and prepared for the day," Rick stated.

"And remember, separation is in preparation and everything happens twice – first in your mind, then in reality. If you can conceive it and believe it, you can achieve it... if you are willing to put in the work."

CHAPTER 19
Elite Mindset Skill #8
Emotional Intelligence

"The eighth skill of an elite mindset is emotional intelligence," Rick said. "It's a combination of self-awareness, self-management, social awareness and relationship management. It is a skill I'm working hard at developing. I'm also reading *Emotional Intelligence 2.0* by Travis Bradberry and Jean Greaves. That's been eye-opening for me.

"I believe, as a leader, that the better emotional intelligence I can develop the better I can serve others. People like people who are like them; if I can increase my social intelligence, I can better connect with others.

"Building connection will make them feel more comfortable with my presence and thus, I can have more impact and influence in helping them become the best versions of themselves and in achieving elite results."

"I could really level up on emotional intelligence," I admitted. "I've struggled recently, more than ever actually, with connecting with all the different types of personalities we have at Bella Medical. We have people right out of college in their early 20's and veterans in the business who are in their 60's. It takes an elite mindset and an equally elite skill set to succeed in executive leadership these days."

"I agree 100%, Mr. Stoneridge," Rick replied. "Developing your emotional intelligence skills might be the fast track to better connection, and better connection is the foundation of leadership. That better connection helps facilitate trust, and leadership is built on trust."

As we walked through the gate to the backyard at my house, I was blown away at how fast the last hour had gone. I hadn't experienced the vortex of evaporating time that comes with being immersed in the moment in a long time. It was fun and invigorating to experience that again.

"Thank you for inviting me, Rick. I truly enjoyed our time together and thank you for sharing the eight skills that make up an elite mindset."

"Well, Mr. Stoneridge, the pleasure was all mine and the joy was all Jersey's." Rick laughed as he unhooked Jersey's harness and she jumped into the swimming pool and swam to the steps to cool off. "That's part of her routine."

We shared a laugh and I thanked Rick for his time, then walked him to the gate.

As I headed back into the pool house, I felt a newly found peace. I felt like I had some strategies to deploy that could help me navigate the next three days of my quarantine. Or should I say the next one day, three times.

CHAPTER 20
What's that Noise?

After a night of reflection on what Rick and I had talked about, I drifted off to sleep, mentally rehearsing what I wanted the next day to look like.

I didn't expect to wake up to the sound of leaf blowers, lawn mowers and chainsaws.

It was 8:30am. I hadn't slept that late in a long time, typically leaving the house by 7:00am so I'd have enough time to stop and get a coffee on my way into the office for our 8:00am start.

I had decided to sleep in as long as possible and had set an alarm for 8:30am. My alarm was typically more sunshine and roses than mowers and blowers.

I walked outside and saw an army of people working away on our property.

One guy was pushing a mower while another was weed-whacking. One was up in the trees trimming branches, another was spreading mulch, and one was cleaning out the sprinkler system.

"Mr. Stoneridge, is that you?" a masked woman asked as she kept her social distance.

"Yes, ma'am. Good morning. Please call me Michael."

"Well, I didn't expect to see you here. I'm TT with TT's Trees and Landscape Company. I hope we didn't wake you. Typically when we come at 8:30am nobody's here so we like to get in, get the job done and get out to stay out of y'all's way," TT explained.

"It's no problem. I'm home on quarantine for the next two days and was just getting up to start my workday," I replied.

"Don't worry about us, Mr. Stoneridge. We will be in and out as quickly as we can be, but not so quickly that we can't do an excellent job," TT said. "How you do anything is how you do everything, and excellence is the standard for our team."

CHAPTER 21
The Team

"Your team is pretty impressive, TT," I commented as I watched the workers move in unison around the yard doing their jobs with precision and intention, communicating more like a group of elite special operations warriors simulating a mission than like a landscape team. They used hand signals, whistles and seemed to be having a great time, all working with a smile and endless energy.

"I appreciate the compliment, sir," TT replied. "We take a lot of pride in working as a team, and we also get a lot of training in how to be a team. At TT's Trees and Landscape, TEAM stands for Together Everyone Achieves More and Total Effort All Members. All we ask for, is all you got. If you give all you got, that's enough for us."

"TT, are you the owner of the company? Is it named after you?" I asked.

"Well, yes and no," TT said with a laugh. "My real name is Julia. The actual owners of the company are Tammy and Trisha. I go by TT because as leaders in the field, we are trained to take ownership – to take ownership of everything from results in service, to our customers' attitudes when we are around. I go by TT because it's a way for me to feel more like an owner of the company when I'm at work. I like it. It allows me to separate the who and the do.

"The *who* I am outside of work is when I wear my Julia hat, and *what* I do at work is my TT hat. I also love the leadership training that Tammy and Trisha give all of our team members: to act as if you are the president of the company and to act as if your job is the most important job in the world. Not to act as if you are the most important *person* in the world, which we need to retrain some of our team members on consistently, but to act as if you have the most important *job* in the world. This mindset allows you to pay attention to detail, to know how to prepare for a great day's work, to give your best effort on every aspect of the job, and to act and work with great discipline."

I was blown away at TT's ownership spirit, at how she could recall what she learned in her training about her leadership presence.

As we continued our conversation and her team worked like a well-oiled machine, I began to notice something that didn't add up.

CHAPTER 22
What's in a Logo?

"TT, what's that in your logo?" I asked. She and her team all had a logo that reflected 8 C's interlocking like a chain link in a circle.

"Oh, that's our company logo. We wear it as a reminder of the 8 C's of Leadership that Tammy and Trisha train each of their team members on when they join the team." TT pointed to the logo on her shirt. "When you join the team at TT's Trees and Landscape, you instantly become a leader. Leaders are trained, not born, so we invest in the training of our team members' leadership skills.

"When you join the team, we have a mindset of what makes you a leader: If anyone is relying on you for anything, you are a leader. The way we work together, we are constantly relying on each other so that makes each of us a leader."

I loved what TT was saying. Much like Rick, what she said made so much sense. She was also bringing the juice.

"Michael, I'm sorry to keep talking your ear off. I just get so excited when I talk about TT's Trees and Landscape; I love the company and love the people. It's such a big part of my life," TT said.

"TT, it's invigorating to hear you talk about your team and your work that way. I wish I had people on my team who cared as much about what we did as you do about your job," I remarked. "I just don't know how to get them inspired or how to get them to take ownership."

"Well, Michael," TT said. "Let me tell you that you're the problem."

CHAPTER 23
The Problem Isn't the Problem;
You're the Problem.

"With all due respect, sir – and please don't take this the wrong way – what I am going to say here isn't going to be easy for me to do," TT said. "I want you to trust my intent. It's coming from a good place, a well-thought-out place, and I have your best interest at heart. Although this conversation might be difficult, I know in the end it will be beneficial for you to hear what I'm going to say. Do I have permission to speak freely, sir?"

Taken aback somewhat by her forwardness, she had my full attention and full permission to speak freely.

"Of course," I replied.

"Michael, whether it's you, Mrs. Stoneridge or any of the people you lead in your job, the problem is never the problem. How you handle the problem is always the problem. Since it's you that's handling the problem, you are part of the problem.

"The best part about you being part of the problem is that you're also part of the solution, but to be part of the solution you must take full ownership and you must take responsibility for more than your direct duties. You must take responsibility for your team's performance as well because if a member of your team is accountable, you are accountable also. You are a team.

"The best teams in sports don't always win and the best businesses don't always get the business. I'd like to think that TT's Trees and Landscape is the best in New York, but we don't get every job. However, we focus on the jobs we have and know that the best way to get more business is to over-deliver in the business we do have.

"We like to look at our customers as clients for life. Once we get into your yard, we want to get into your life and be much more than a tree and landscape service. We want to create the safe, clean, immaculate backyard of your dreams where you can enjoy making good memories."

"TT, all I can say is thank you. Thank you for your honesty, your ownership and your leadership," I said. "I've been needing to hear what you have to say and I want to know more. May I ask you about the 8 C's of Leadership?"

CHAPTER 24
Pillar #2 – Elite Leadership & The 8 C's of Leadership

"Of course you can!" TT responded. "The 8 C's of Leadership are part of our elite results system. They are part of our training and are like a ticket to admission to the team. You can't join the team until you have memorized the 8 C's of Leadership. We have our team members memorize the 8 C's because we want them to take ownership of the team, and taking ownership follows a three-step process.

"Step one is you know it; that's why we do the extensive training. Step two is you do it; that's why we have a point person on every team. Today that's me. Step three is to own it. You can't own it until you know it and do it enough, so that it becomes a part of you."

"Know it, do it, own it. I love that, TT!" I exclaimed. "What are the 8 C's? I'm dying to know."

"Michael, you are home on quarantine. Are you dying? Do you need me to call 9-1-1?" TT asked with a laugh. "I'm just kidding. Let me give you the 8 C's – the 8 Skills of Leadership that we train at TT's – and let me do it swiftly so that we can get to our next job on time, but slowly enough so that you understand and are able to start building the 8 C's of Leadership skill set in yourself.

Remember, it has to be in you before it shows up in what you do."

CHAPTER 25
Elite Leadership Skill #1
Connection

"The first of the 8 C's, or what we also call The 8 Skills of Elite Leadership, is the skill of Connection," TT said as she interlocked her hands, making a hand signal for connection. "Connection is the foundation of trust and is built from time together and often through shared adversity. We like to work hard together and through that work, we build bonds together. We also invest a lot of time together and that helps build a connection on the team."

As I reflected on my current position at work and at home, connection was something I felt like I was missing. There was a time that connection was my strength, but as I keep getting promoted and making more money, having more responsibility and traveling more, I felt like I was losing connection with my team at Bella Medical and with Amelia and Rhys.

"When I was first hired by TT's, I went to dinner with Tammy and Trisha. At the time I was working for one of the other landscapers in town. It was funny, but the night before I had gone to dinner with the owner of that company, Joseph Cooper, who's a great guy. When I was at dinner with the man they call "Coop" and other members of the team, I was constantly reminded of his greatness," TT said. "I was reminded of how successful he was and how great the company was.

"The next night when I was at dinner with Tammy and Trisha, they reminded me of the greatness that's inside of me. They reminded me of how great I was for the company. It was like the night before I was in the presence of greatness and then the next night, *I* was greatness. Tammy and Trisha made me feel like I was the most important person in the room, where the night before I felt like the owner of the company was the most important person in the room.

"Tammy and Trisha really tuned into WIIFM and that stuck out to me. It helped deepen a connection very quickly."

"WIIFM. What's that?" I asked.

"What's In It For Me." TT smiled and continued: "They were very clear about what was in it for me. They wanted to make sure I saw the growth opportunities available for me if I joined the team, versus the bottom line for the owner and company. The best thing I've taken from Tammy and Trisha is that if you want more, you must become more. And the best part about them is that they make the investment to help you become more, to become the best version of yourself.

"The connection that they make is a reflection of their second C."

CHAPTER 26
Elite Leadership Skill #2
Character

"As great as they are at connection, I think their greatest skill is Character. Who they are and how they live," TT said as she made a hand motion of someone looking inside of herself. "They are more concerned with doing right than being right. They are intentional about living out of principle versus preference.

"Too many leaders let emotion dictate how they lead, or let how they feel dictate how they act. Not Tammy and Trisha. They let their core principles, not their preferences, guide their behavior."

Principle over preference, doing what's right versus being right. I loved those two aspects of the skill of character.

"TT, Tammy and Trisha sound like amazing leaders. Very cool that you get to work with them."

"They are, for sure," TT agreed. "Don't get me wrong – they aren't perfect. They make mistakes, but when they do, they own them and work to make the next best decision and do the next right thing.

"That's what they train us to do as team members. They train us to own our behavior, to own our decisions, to say what we see, and to trust the intent of our teammates. If we get it wrong or make a mistake, we subsequently put all of our energy into making the next best decision and doing the next best thing for our team and our customers."

CHAPTER 27
Elite Leadership Skill #3
Consistency

"The third C, the third skill of elite leadership, is Consistency." TT moved her hand up and down like she was rhythmically bouncing a basketball.

"Look, anyone can be good once in a while. But we don't want to be a one-hit wonder and we don't want to be temporary. We want to be legendary, and to be legendary you have to be consistent as a leader. If you want legendary results, you need to bring legendary consistency to your performance. Consistency is trained. Just like working a chain saw or a weed-whacker, anyone can do it with the right training."

I was quickly becoming convinced that training was the key to leadership, that leadership was a skill that could be trained. I had never heard anyone speak about leadership like that and it was refreshing to know that I could level up my leadership if I leveled up my training.

"What I'm hearing you say, TT, is that leadership can be trained. That you're not born a leader but you become a leader?"

"That's correct," TT said. "People think life is a talent game, that leadership is some inherent talent that people are born with, but it's not. It's a trainable skill.

"We like to say at TT's Trees and Landscape that life is a strategy-and-training game, not a talent-and-genes game. You aren't born a leader or born able to connect, have character or be a machine of consistency. You're trained in those skills, just like you are trained in the fourth C."

CHAPTER 28
Elite Leadership Skill #4
Communication

"The fourth skill or the fourth C of elite leadership is Communication," TT said as she made a talking-mouth motion with her hand. "Communication is one of the most underdeveloped skills we have as people these days and it's why we don't allow cell phones on the job."

This piqued my interest. I felt like my entire job was done glued to a cell phone.

"You don't allow cell phones on the job?" I asked.

"No, sir. We want team members to communicate with each other using hand signals if it's loud and using words, eye contact and body language when possible. Obviously, being masked up and socially distant has provided an additional layer of challenge to our communication, but we embrace that challenge and combat it with more communication training," TT answered.

"We found that when we removed cell phones from our job sites, our team members became more concerned and focused on the opinions of the five people they are working with every day than the 500 people online that they didn't even know.

"As the team point person, I like to take before and after photos of our work to show our progress and document our works of art, but that's all we use a cell phone for on the job. We want to eliminate the distractions we can control and create boundaries so we can stay focused on the job at hand and be where our feet are. This helps us in executing the fifth C."

CHAPTER 29
Elite Leadership Skill #5
Clarity

"When you improve communication, the result is improved Clarity," TT stated, raising her hands up as if they were glasses she was looking through. "When a leader can create clarity – clarity of purpose, clarity of task, clarity of each person's share of the task – it increases ownership and increases speed of execution.

"The one thing we can't get more of is time. The sun sets every day; we can't hit a target that we can't see and we can't do our job when it's so dark we cannot see. Life's the same way. If you lack clarity of purpose or clarity of your objective, you get paralyzed by indecision and you spin your wheels. Spinning your wheels might look like work, but in reality it's not."

I took a deep breath. As I exhaled, I was reminded of how much I felt like I had been spinning my wheels. I wasn't clear with my goals and certainly wasn't clear with my purpose.

"You know, Michael, I have found that each of the 8 C's, the 8 Skills of Elite Leadership, build on top of each other like a Venn diagram, or like your yard. The sprinkler system feeds the grass, which holds the water for the trees, which provide a place for the flowers to bloom and the birds to live.

"A yard is like one big ecosystem working together synergistically so that all can benefit, similar to how elite teams are run and how elite leaders lead.

"Each part of the ecosystem knows its role and executes for the team. Just like on our team, each person has a specialized skill set and that skill set is part of the sixth C of leadership."

CHAPTER 30
Elite Leadership Skill #6
Competence

"That specialized skill set is what we call Competence, the sixth skill of elite leadership," TT said as she stuck her hand in the air doing her Jordan impersonation, a logo known best as *Jumpman*.

"Competence is your ability to get results, to do a job. As on any team, certain people are better at certain jobs than others. You have to put people where they will shine, not where they will whine."

"I love that, TT," I responded. "Put your people where they will shine, not where they will whine."

"Yes. It's funny; there is a concept called the Peter Principle where people rise to their level of incompetence. They get one promotion after another until they are in a job where they don't have the competent skill set needed to execute their duties properly. The result is they get frustrated and the company's growth stalls because the right person is in the wrong position. I saw this all the time in my previous life working in pharmaceutical sales. Tammy and Trisha are very intentional about who, how and when they promote so that we don't get blindsided by the Peter Principle."

The Peter Principle. I had never heard of it before and now felt like I was living it. I'd been promoted right before this pandemic hit and was now in a role that required lots of communication via technology. Technology wasn't a strong skill set of mine; neither was patience. Come to think of it, my favorite position I ever had at Bella Medical was when I was in an assistant/supportive role where I supported and helped make decisions versus being the one who everyone turned to for decisions. Amelia had told me once that it was like I was living in a state of decision fatigue, and maybe this was why. I was better at carrying out decisions than making them.

"When you find out what you are good at and competent in, and you can do that and see results, you find joy. It's hard to find joy in frustration – frustration that comes from being tasked to do a job you're not trained to do. It's much easier to turn that frustration into fascination and get excited about work every day when you are working in an area where you have competence," TT said.

"Competence can also be a curse if you're not challenged to stretch and grow. It's like Goldilocks. If it's too easy or too hard, we check out. If it's the right level of challenge, we check in, and when we check in, it's easier to develop the seventh C."

CHAPTER 31
Elite Leadership Skill #7
Commitment

"Commitment happens when you are challenged to grow and you find that challenge at the right level, like Goldilocks," TT continued as she made a motion of putting a ring on her finger. "The biggest challenge I see with leading and hiring is that people like to be a part of a team when it's convenient versus being committed.

"They like being a part of a team when it serves them versus showing up to serve the team. At TT's Trees and Landscape, we challenge our team members to commit to serving their team or to quit. Commit or quit.

"We want team members who work out of conviction instead of convenience. You can't just show up when it's convenient; you have to show up all the time.

"You can't just show up when you feel like it. You have to be committed and know that when you show up, THEN you will feel like it.

"The show-up comes before the feeling. It's like starting an exercise program – the hardest part is the start. It's the start that stops most people. The feeling doesn't come first; the commitment comes first and feeling follows.

"We had a speaker at our annual conference this year who was amazing. She is World Champion in Rodeo. Her name is Donene Taylor and her book, *Heart of a Champion*, is one of the best I've ever read.

"In the book she talks about the skill of continually choosing to commit to your commitments. I thought that was awesome and had never heard it put like that."

"That's gold. Commit to your commitments," I said. "I am going to have to bring her in to speak to my team. We need to recommit to our commitments."

"Well, Michael, getting commitment from others starts with committing to yourself," TT responded. "Recommitting to your commitments daily is a necessity because of all the distractions that can slow down our actions in the busy world we live in. If you want a more committed team, you need to be a more committed leader. If you're going to be a more committed leader, that takes the eighth skill of the 8 C's of elite leadership."

CHAPTER 32
Elite Leadership Skill #8
Courage

"Courage is the skill of doing what needs to be done regardless of how you feel. It's like being fearless as a leader, but being fearless doesn't exist. Courage is acting in the face of fear, not the absence of fear. Anyone can act in absence of fear, but it's the courageous leaders who still take action when they have fear," TT said as she made a hand signal of a gun.

"I've been making these hand signals, Michael, as a way to give you a visual reminder of the 8 C's, and I use a gun for courage because people in law enforcement and the military who carry guns do courageous feats every day. They are the ones who go running into action when everyone else goes running away. They don't run in because they are fearless; they run in because they are courageous and they know that if it's not them, then who?"

One of my teammates in college became a fireman and I always admired his courage; he literally ran into burning buildings risking his life to save people he didn't even know.

"I love that description of courage, TT," I said. "Acting in the face of fear versus the absence of fear."

"Yes, so do I," TT replied. "I've learned to use fear as fuel, that fear is a healthy emotion because you know what the outcome can be. You just have to learn how to process it properly. At TT's Trees and Landscape we teach that FEAR is an acronym for False Evidence Appearing Real, that our fears are often made up in our minds and if we make them, we can break them. When you admit your fears, you zap them of their control over your behaviors and you start to talk to yourself about what to do, and your next best move versus listening to that voice of fear. We like to call it the winner voice versus the whiner voice."

I had been listening to my whiner voice a lot more than my winner voice recently and I knew that needed to change if I was going to improve my performance at work and at home.

CHAPTER 33
Never Goodbye, *Always* See You Later

"Well, Michael, it's time for us to head to our next job. It's been great meeting you. I've enjoyed chatting with you about the 8 C's, the 8 Skills of Elite Leadership," TT said. "We never say *goodbye*; we always say *see you later*. It's a mindset that leaders have about remembering tomorrow, that you will see each other again."

"Well, TT... I've enjoyed it," I said with a smile. Before you go, may we please review the 8C's of leadership and your hand signals to help me conceptualize and remember them?"

"Of course." TT then made the following hand signals as I recalled the skills.

TT's hand signal for skill #1: hands together.

"Connection," I answered.

TT's hand signal for skill #2: pulling her jacket or chest open as she looked inside.

"Character."

TT's hand signal for skill #3: a motion of dribbling a basketball.

"Consistency."

TT's hand signal for skill #4: making the motion of a talking mouth.

"Communication."

TT's hand signal for skill #5: circular hands over her eyes.

"Clarity."

TT's hand signal for skill #6: her best Jordan impersonation.

"Competence."

TT's hand signal for skill #7: putting a ring on her ring finger.

"Commitment."

TT's hand signal for skill #8: a gun sign.

"Courage."

"Bravo, Michael – 8 for 8! That was great," TT said. "See you later, sir."

TT ran out of the gate to join her team at the trucks, while I stood there shocked that I could recall all eight of the Skills of Elite Leadership so easily.

I turned around and walked back into the pool house. Sitting at my computer, I felt better than I had in years. There was a feeling of clarity, of purpose, a feeling of hope.

Then I looked over at the photos of my family on the wall. Beside one of the photos was another quote that I hadn't noticed yet in my new place of office and residence:

HOPE – Hold On, Possibilities Exist

I smiled. For the first time in a long time I felt like my luck was turning, that I was finding a little motivation, a little juice to do what needed to be done.

"If you're juiceful, you're useful," I said out loud with a chuckle. Then I opened up my laptop and went to work.

CHAPTER 34
No Decision Is a Decision

Later that day I realized that I had worked with a focus, a purpose and a service mindset that had been missing for a long time.

When Amelia and Rhys got home, they came over to the pool house, albeit they stayed in the doorway properly social distancing.

When they showed up, I closed my laptop so I could be where my feet were. I was more present and it was as if you could feel their presence.

Not long after conversing in the doorway, Rhys went chasing after Jerz as Amelia and I watched.

Amelia asked me how it was going. Much to her surprise, I told her how I had enjoyed being home and how I had learned a lot from Rick and from Julia of TT's Trees and Landscape.

She corrected me and said that her name was TT. We both agreed how unique and cool it was that she had this alter ego.

I reviewed the 8 C's, the 8 Skills of Leadership with Amelia and also what I had learned from Rick about mindset.

She then asked me a very pointed question.

"What are you going to do with all of this, Michael? What changes are you going to make? Knowledge isn't power. Knowledge is nothing without action. It's action that changes everything. You need to make a decision about what you are going to do and remember, no decision is a decision. This quarantine may be a blessing in disguise for you, for us and for your Bella Medical career. It's up to you to decide. You evolve or become extinct. Your decisions determine your destiny. No decision is a decision, Michael," Amelia repeated.

"Rhys and I are going to let you be so you have your space to continue to reflect and refocus and use this time to your advantage, and to make the most of this time you've been gifted."

As Amelia walked away and closed the pool house door behind her, I paused before reopening my laptop and getting back to my inbox. And I asked myself:

What do I really want?
What changes do I need to make?
Who is it that I want to become?

I knew that the better the questions you ask yourself the better your life becomes. I just had forgotten to ask myself any questions other than *Why is this happening to me?*

It was time for a change. I just wasn't sure exactly what changes I needed to make.

CHAPTER 35
Walking Jersey and Reflection

The next morning, I woke up and decided to go for a walk, thinking it would be fun to bring Jerz with me as a form of patience training. Usually, I was so focused on my workout for the day and about everything I had to get done that the last thing I wanted was to have to slow down for my old four-legged friend.

This morning, though, I thought maybe she could teach me a thing or two about patience and enjoying the finer things in life such as a walk, smelling a bush or being fascinated by simpler things – like the squirrels and ducks that she continually wanted to chase after.

As we walked, I continued to reflect on what I had learned from Rick, from TT, and from my short yet impactful conversation with Amelia.

After all, Amelia had a way with words. She was a music teacher and one of the best songwriters I'd ever known. Come to think of it, she was the only songwriter I had ever known, but she was a damn good one.

I reflected on the 8 Skills of an Elite Mindset and the main points I had taken away:

- Be where your feet are.
- Remember tomorrow.
- Flip the switch.

I reflected on the 8 Skills of Elite Leadership:

1. Connection
2. Character
3. Consistency
4. Communication
5. Clarity
6. Competence
7. Commitment
8. Courage

I was feeling educated, empowered and energized.

I was ready to make some better decisions, chart my course for how I wanted to come out of this quarantine refocused, re-energized and ready to dominate the day.

When Jerz and I got back home, I unhooked her harness and she jumped in the pool. Routine.

As I walked toward the pool house, laughing at her consistency and vibrance for life and simplicity, I was shocked at what I saw next.

CHAPTER 36
Sandy's Sanitation Services

"Hello... Hello... HELLO!!!!" I shouted louder each time.

A person dressed in a hazmat suit, who looked more like an astronaut than someone from a cleaning service company, turned around and waved.

She had been spraying the countertops and table surfaces in the pool house with a disinfectant spray and then wiping them down with a towel.

As she approached me and walked outside the pool house, she spoke with the muffled sound you would expect to hear from someone dressed in a suit like that.

"Mr. Stoneridge, do I have permission to remove my helmet now that I'm outside?" she asked.

"Of course," I answered. "And please, call me Michael."

"Thank you, Michael," the woman said as she took off her helmet. She still had a mask on and made sure to keep her distance. "Hi. I'm Sandy from Sandy's Sanitation Services. Mrs. Stoneridge asked that I come and sanitize the pool house and then the house in anticipation of you finishing your quarantine and returning to the house with her and Rhys. I've been cleaning your house for four years since you all moved in. I think this is the first time we've met. It's nice to finally put a face to a name, Michael."

I couldn't believe it. Here I was meeting yet another person for the first time who had been in my house during the last four years and knew my wife and daughter. What had happened to me during those years? Was I really that busy and disconnected?

"It's nice to meet you too, Sandy," I said.

"I won't be long, sir. Finishing up here in the pool house and then going to do the main house so that everything is sanitized, safe and secure for your welcome home party," Sandy said with a chuckle. "Don't be alarmed by my outfit. We take extra precautions and believe it's always better to be safe than sorry, especially when working during a global pandemic.

"It's our mission to leave the world a cleaner and safer place so that our customers can live their best lives. Pandemic or no-demic, we strive for integrity, cleanliness and kindness in all we do. It's in our culture. It's what we do. It's who we are."

Sandy used a phrase that caught my attention. She said, "It's in our culture." I knew we had a culture and a mission statement at Bella Medical. I didn't know what they were without looking, and I for sure wasn't on a mission or contributing much to our corporate culture based on the feedback I had gotten from Robert Coachman before beginning my quarantine.

I needed to know more about this culture and mission of Sandy's.

"Sandy, you just said two words that hit me – *mission* and *culture*. What do you mean by *it's our mission* and *it's in our culture*?" I asked.

"Well, Michael, at Sandy's Sanitation Services we believe that culture isn't just a thing. We believe that culture is everything," Sandy said, perking up a bit from her already perky state. "Our culture is a set of beliefs that drive our behaviors, what we do and what we don't do, how we act, how we treat each other, how we treat our customers, how we do our jobs. We intentionally create a culture because our culture is, again, what drives our behaviors and it's our behaviors that produce our results.

"We live in a results-driven world and if you want to produce elite results, you must first start with producing an elite culture."

Culture drives behavior and behavior drives results. Sandy made that sound so simple.

"Sandy, how did you all go about establishing and then enhancing your company culture?"

"Michael, I'm glad you asked," Sandy replied. "It's actually much easier than you might think to get started, but it's a journey that never ends; your culture is ALWAYS under construction.

"Also, you either get the culture you create or get the culture that unintentionally forms, an want to play offense as leaders and be intentional with how we establish our culture.

"Nothing good happens by accident; it only happens by intention. We start with being intentional about establishing our mission so that our team members can be on a mission.

"We don't just want to have a mission statement; we want people who are on a mission."

CHAPTER 38

Elite Culture Skill #1
Mission

"In order to be on a mission, you first have to create a mission statement. It starts on paper and then must get into the minds, hearts and behaviors of your team members," Sandy stated. "Our mission is to *leave the world a cleaner and safer place so that our customers can live their best lives.*"

"How did you come up with that mission, Sandy?"

She responded, "As the owner of the company, I started by asking myself, 'What do I want the gravestone for this company to be? What do I want people to say about us when we are gone, literally and figuratively?'

"I brainstormed with some of our team members and we decided that if we left the world a cleaner and safer place, our customers could live their best lives. If we were helping our customers live their best lives, then our job was very meaningful due to the impact it had in the marketplace and on people. People are our marketplace and our mission statement helps us remember the *why* behind doing what we do."

I could connect with what Sandy was saying about the importance of connecting to her *why*, to being on a mission. It felt like I had lost sight of my mission and why I was at Bella Medical in the first place other than it was a job that paid my bills and afforded my family a nice house to live in. However, since I was traveling on a weekly basis, I was not really living there anyway. I needed to get back on a mission.

I was also a bit confused. Neither Sandy nor TT nor Rick had talked about making money. It was like they were philosophical nomads who did their jobs at an elite level and loved their jobs, but they never talked about money. I was wanting to know where results and the bottom line came into the mission.

"Sandy, what about results? What about being profitable as a company? How do you reflect the importance of that in your mission?" I asked.

"I'm glad you asked. That's the next step in establishing and enhancing an elite culture," she replied. "After you identify your mission, you go to work to create your vision."

CHAPTER 39
Elite Culture Skill #2
Vision

"You know, Michael, the mission is essentially our *why*. The vision is our *what* – what we want to earn, what we want to do," Sandy continued. "Think about mission as your philosophical why and a race that has no finish line. Your vision is your resume – your scoreboard if you will and your numbers that you measure against. It's what you project and then produce. Your vision has clear finish lines and can be measured clearly. After all, measurement is motivation and you measure what you treasure.

"Part of our vision is to be a $10MM/year profitable company. In order to do that we reverse engineer the vision to be a $2.5MM/quarter company, and then within that quarter an $850K/month profitable company. We even go as far as breaking that down to $215K per week and $55K per day since we only operate four days a week. We go hard so we can give our team members three-day weekends, Saturday/Sunday/Monday, and be recharged and ready to ride Tuesday–Friday.

"As a leadership group, we take Monday to get our plans mapped out for the week and use Saturday and Sunday to unplug from work and plug into our families.

"It's a formula and a vision that's worked for us. We've been a $10MM+ profitable company for the last decade and with this pandemic, business is only getting better. We've had to pivot and adapt and adjust, but that's life. You get lemons, you make lemonade. It's that simple."

Sandy made it sound so easy.

Mission was why.

Vision was what.

Mission was philosophical.

Vision was tangible.

As a collegiate athlete, I was always a goal setter and a goal getter. Now, at 40 years old and with the same company for 18 years, I was more on a treadmill of going through the motions rather than growing from the motions.

"Sandy, I love how you separate and define mission and vision. What else do you do to help build your organizational culture?"

CHAPTER 40
Elite Culture Skill #3
Core Principles

"Well, we start with clarifying the mission and the vision so that everyone knows why we do what we do and what we want to accomplish," Sandy answered. "The next step, and it goes hand in hand with the mission and vision, is to identify our organizational core principles, our core values.

"We refer to them as core principles so that we can identify our culture with an MVP process: Mission, Vision, Principles.

"Our core principles are HOW we do what we do, and HOW we behave. HOW we act, behave and live, gives us the best chance for success in achieving our goals. Again, the mission is WHY we do what we do. The vision is WHAT we want to accomplish.

"Our core principles are ICK. We thought it was fitting because when homeowners see something at their house and say 'ick,' we want them to call Sandy's Sanitation so we can *lick the ick*," Sandy said with a smile. "It's our way of remembering our core principles of Integrity, Cleanliness and Kindness.

"One of the biggest challenges in developing our team members is getting them to live out of principles versus out of preference. When you live out of preference, you do what you feel like doing. When you live out of principles, you preset your mindset to live a certain way; you pre-commit to what you will do and what you won't do. It's our version of a crockpot, only for us it's 'set it and don't forget it.' It's about living, working and serving with integrity, cleanliness and kindness so we can achieve our vision and execute our mission."

My head was about to explode. Not explode with overwhelm, but to explode with excitement. Sandy made it so simple.

Identify your mission, your why.

Create your vision, your what.

Live by your core principles, your how.

"Sandy, does this just work for corporations or can you establish an MVP process like this for an individual?" I asked.   "I think that having a personal MVP process could be very beneficial for me in helping to create my future."

"Michael, YES!!!" Sandy exclaimed.   "The MVP process is a lifestyle, not an event. It's not something that's restricted to just a team or corporation; it's something that I believe each individual needs to explore and create for himself or herself. If individuals can have and live by their personal MVP process, it only becomes easier for them to do it on an organizational level as a part of a team that's bigger than themselves.

"The challenge for most people is the start. As we say, it's the start that stops most people and you can't let the start stop you.   Michael, let's get started by identifying your one-word brand."

CHAPTER 41
Elite Culture Skill #4
The One-Word Brand

"To get started with creating their own personal MVP process or a set of core principles, I'll often ask our team members to give me their one-word brand," Sandy said. "The one-word brand is so simple, yet so powerful. Let me ask you this, Michael, just as I would one of our new team members:

"What is one word that, for the rest of this quarter, this three-month segment, would help you close the gap from where you are to where you want to be personally and professionally? The one word that anyone who interacted with you – your wife, your daughter, people on your team at work – would say, 'You know, that Michael Stoneridge, he sure is ____.' What is the word they would use?"

Man, I had never thought about that. A one-word brand, a one-word core principle. I had never been that intentional. And then it hit me...

"*Intention!*" I exclaimed. "I'd want my one word to be *intention*. If I am more intentional at home and in the office, it will improve my relationships and that's important for me right now."

"Not only would being more intentional improve your relationships," Sandy said, "it would also

improve your results.   Improving relationships
with ourselves, our family, our teams ALWAYS
precedes improved results. I think intention is a
great word for you, sir. I've used that one before
and it was really beneficial. My one-word brand
right now is *why*, because when we have a big
enough why, we can always, always find a way
how.

"Michael, may I tell you a story?"

CHAPTER 42
Elite Culture Skill #5
Reveal Your Why

"A few years ago, during horse racing season at the Boser Racetrack in Boser Springs, New York, there was a county fair and at the fair was a big, muscular strongman," Sandy said as she dug in to tell her story. "He was performing some amazing feats of strength on stage. To the amazement of the crowd he was ripping decks of cards in half, bending steel with his hands – it was impressive!

"In one of his acts, he pulled out a lemon and with his big, strong hands, he squeezed out all the juice from that lemon and said, 'Ladies and gentlemen, I am a strongman. I've squeezed all of the juice out of this lemon. I will give $1,000 to anyone who can come up and extract one more drop.'

"In response to his challenge two giant men went on stage to give it a try. The first guy grabbed the lemon and gave it a good, hard squeeze. No drop. The crowd laughed in amusement as he stepped back to let his friend try.

"The crowd went silent and watched as the second guy gave the lemon a squeeze, contorting his face in grimaced concentration. He suddenly

103

released his grip with a gasp for air, but still, not one drop of juice came out of that lemon.

"The crowd laughed and applauded as the two men exited the stage. The strongman was left on stage holding his arms in the air with the lemon in his hand when he saw an older woman, who looked to be in her seventies, walking up the stairs onto the stage.

"The strongman said, 'Ma'am, for the sake of time, can we move on? You aren't going to squeeze any juice out of this lemon. I mean, c'mon, the two guys who just tried couldn't do it and they looked like professional football players.'

"Sir, just give me a chance," the woman said politely. "I have a big reason WHY."

"Okay, here you go. One chance," said the strongman, who handed her the lemon as the crowd cheered in support.

"The woman took the lemon in her hands and began to squeeze. Her face became contorted. Her jaw set. Her veins began popping out of her forehead. Her glasses fell off her face. Her entire body shook back and forth from her intense struggle with the lemon as she squeezed it with all her might.

"And then... BOOM!! Out came one drop of juice.

"The audience erupted in applause! The sounds of clapping, whistles and cheers rang throughout the fair and the nearby Boser Springs Racetrack. The strongman was blown away as he was compelled to show the audience the plate on which the drop of lemon juice had fallen. The woman stood there onstage with her hands on her knees as she collected her breath. It was a scene to behold.

"The strongman walked over with a check he had just written out for $1,000 and handed it to the woman. Then he said, 'Ma'am, you have got to tell us how you did it. In all my years of doing this, I've never had anyone squeeze an extra drop of juice out of a lemon. How did you do it?'

"She replied, 'Sir, I'm 74 years old, I just lost my husband, I have three grandchildren that we're raising, and I just lost my job. I needed that money to feed and care for my grandchildren.'

"The woman was inspired. She was motivated. She had revealed her WHY! She needed to squeeze that juice out of the lemon to feed and take care of her grandchildren, and with a big enough reason why, you will always, ALWAYS find a way how. Your reason why is the fuel that burns the fire of inspiration and motivation inside of you.

"Michael, you must tap into your why. What's your why? Why do you do what you do? Why are you working in the job you do? Why are you living in this home right now? You must ask yourself *Why?*"

Wow... All I could think was *wow*. As I wiped a tear from my eye, the emotion of the story and the big why the older woman had for her grandchildren hit me. I was not as present as I wanted to be while Rhys was growing up in her first 10 years of life. I always said I would make more time when I did this or accomplished that, and Amelia had reminded me of the disease of "When I..." – the disease that comes because you always put off what you should do until a day that never comes. I was regretting that more than I had thought.

"Sandy, that's a great story. I'm not sure I know my why, but it's something I need to tap into," I said with a crack in my voice. "My why is my baby girl Rhys and my wife Amelia. I just haven't been as present, intentional or good at it as I want to be or as I need to be."

And with that, more tears started to roll down my cheek. As I wiped them away in hopes that

Sandy wouldn't see them, she leaned forward and in a soft and assuring voice she said:

"Maybe not as intentional or present as you have wanted to be or have needed to be. GOOD. Now you know where to go to work. Now you know what you need to do.

"I have total confidence and believe in you that you can do it. Remember this most powerful 8-word sentence: *It's going to be; it's up to me.* You can do this, Michael; you can do anything you want with enough time and the right training. But first, you have to identify your non-negotiables and set some boundaries for yourself and your time."

CHAPTER 43
Elite Culture Skill #6
Unyielding Non-Negotiables

"Once you have revealed your why, you know your one-word brand and have identified your mission, vision and core principles, that's just half the battle," Sandy said. "The next step is creating boundaries on what you will and won't do and listing out your unyielding non-negotiables.

"Success is about identifying what you won't do as much as what you will do. It's about creating boundaries on what behaviors you must start but also what you must stop and what you want to continue.

"One of my non-negotiables is to sweat before screens, to work out in the morning before I get on a screen, a laptop, my phone or watch TV. It's non-negotiable for me to invest into myself and take care of Sandy before I do anything else.

"Another non-negotiable for me is no phones at the dinner table. My kids and my husband would sit at the table and text each other versus talk with each other. It was so crazy. Now we have a *no cell phone* standard at the dinner table and it's been fun to see my kids and their father re-engage with each other verbally."

I shook my head. Amelia was always on me about being on my phone at the table and when I was with Rhys. Rhys even asked her mother one day, "Mommy, why is Daddy always on his phone? Does he love his phone more than me?" That about broke my heart, but I hadn't yet broken the habit of having a digital leash around my neck and constantly being connected to my phone.

"Sandy, I do that. Like your husband, I am on my phone all the time. Do you have any non-negotiable standards you can share with me about that?" I asked.

"Sure do. It's funny, Michael," Sandy replied. "In this hyper-connected world of social media, cell phones, Zoom, FaceTime, etc., we are less connected physically, mentally and emotionally than ever. It's why depression rates, suicide rates and anxiety are at an all-time high.

"As humans, we are social creatures. We need healthy social interaction. We are humans, not hermits. To help with this interaction we have implemented a digital sunset in our home. When the sun goes down, our electronics go down with it. Long gone are the years of Dad on his phone, me watching TV and the kids playing video games from dinner to bedtime. We actually engage and interact as a family and have real human conversation and real human connection.

"We started it seven days a week and now it's every other day. My husband and I have continued the digital sunset on those days and it has elevated all aspects of our marriage and relationship. Having that unyielding non-negotiable boundary has been a marriage, family and sanity savior.

"The other additional benefit from all of that uninterrupted time is the opportunity it provides to be creative. We need space to be creative and, in that space, my husband and I found and set our misogi."

"I'm sorry," I said with a confused look on my face. "You found your what?"

CHAPTER 44
Elite Culture Skill #7
Setting Your Misogi

"Not to be confused with The Karate Kid and Mr. Miyagi, or visiting your favorite Polish restaurant and eating a pierogi, we were able to find and set our misogi," Sandy said, laughing. "*Misogi* is an ancient Japanese word that basically means setting a goal that's so hard and so big that when you do it, the misogi positively impacts the other 364 days of your year.

"My husband and I to date have done two misogis together. We ran 100+ miles across the state of Vermont from Massachusetts to Canada and we built a pole barn with a gym, office and golf simulator. At the time we didn't know how to build a barn, golf or work out. It was a goal that took us all year; it brought us together and built us up. It was so much fun and so stinkin' hard!

"The thing about your misogi is that you don't completely publicize it. The challenge is designed by you and for you, and I am only sharing mine with you so you get the idea. I also believe that once you share your misogi with one accountability partner, you are cementing your commitment to doing it. The misogi should also be really, really hard and you should be unsure if you can complete it or not. Part of the challenge is finding out if you can do it.

"I personally like to share it with others because I like being a part of a group, but to each their own. My husband likes to keep his misogi to himself, while I like bringing others into the mix to share the experience with us.

"The bottom line here is this, and it ties directly back to your one-word brand, Michael. You have to have goals and you have to have goals that scare you, challenge you and set your soul on fire. The type of goals that are so big that you need to have a clear why, if you are ever going to find a way how.

"But having a big goal and a clear why might not be enough to get the results you are looking for. You most likely will need the eighth skill of an elite culture if you are going to do what you set out to do organizationally and individually, especially if your goals are big, like climbing Mt. Everest big. If you want to just go summit your local community hill, you don't need any of this. This is for slaying the dragons, for doing things most people don't, and for getting big stuff done that requires you to be at your very best. The type of elite results that elite organizations and elite people pursue. Elite people   like   YOU!"

CHAPTER 45
Elite Culture Skill #8
The Four-Step Success Formula

"Look, wishing doesn't work; work works," Sandy stated. "And speaking of work, Michael, I need to get back to work so you can get back into your newly sanitized house tonight.

"Doing great work requires a great focus because it's your focus that determines your future. All great work follows a four-step success formula. Yeah, you can get lucky and win once in a while on luck, but luck isn't a strategy – just as waiting till you feel like taking action isn't a strategy for action. You have to get started.

"It makes the start easier when you know the four-step success formula.

"Step #1 is to set your intention, to identify what it is you want to do.

"Step #2 is to schedule when you will take action on what you are wanting to do.

"Step #3 is to measure your actions or track your behaviors so you can see how often you actually DWYSYWD – Do What You Said You Would Do.

"Step #4 is to reflect and refocus using a simple system we at Sandy's Sanitation call the start, stop, continue system. At the start of each day, we simply reflect on the last 24 hours of our lives and ask ourselves, 'What must we start, what must we stop and what must we continue to close the gap from where we are to where we want to be?' And then we go to work on doing what we write down for that start, stop, continue.

"We then rinse and repeat the process over and over again, day to day, not counting the days but making the days count till we get the results we are looking for; and then we raise the bar, recalculate, refocus and re-engage towards the next step in our vision or the next misogi or goal we have. It's been a process that has helped us go from being a mom-and-pop sanitation operation to a $10MM annual company that employs 100+ people a year."

"Sandy, you make the process of success and establishing and enhancing an elite culture sound so simple," I commented.

"It is simple," Sandy said. "But don't confuse simple with easy. Just because a process is simple doesn't make it easy. Look, establishing and enhancing an elite culture is simple. Becoming successful is simple. People are complex."

CHAPTER 46
If You Don't Use It, You Lose It

"Michael, I've enjoyed our time chatting today. It's been nice to finally meet you and to get to talk. I've got to get back to my mission here and *leave the world a cleaner and safer place so that our customers can live their best lives*, and that starts with you and your home. I'm all done here in the pool house. Nice place. Not a bad spot to do your quarantine."

"Sandy, thank you. I've enjoyed our time and enjoyed learning about the MVP process, one-word brand, the importance of knowing your why, setting unyielding non-negotiables, having a misogi and the four-step success formula," I replied. "I will be implementing what we talked about today. Thank you."

"Last thing, Michael. If you don't use it, you will lose it," Sandy said. "You have greatness inside of you. Everything you need to succeed is already inside you. Hard times don't last; hard people do. Don't wish your situation were any easier. Instead, work to make yourself so strong, so systematic, to have such an elite mindset, leadership and culture skills that you can endure any pandemic, any adversity and win on any day.

"Michael, it has been a pleasure to meet you and chat with you. Let me leave you with this… When you create a plan and then put your plan to work, you will give yourself the best chance at getting what you want. You have to start with what you want, why you want it, have a plan to get it, and then get after your plan. Dominate the day, Mr. Stoneridge."

And with that, Sandy put her helmet back on and waved as she walked towards and entered the main house.

I walked back into the pool house and sat down in the same place on the couch that I had been all quarantine.

Except in this instance, when I grabbed my laptop...

CHAPTER 47
Plan Your Work, Work Your Plan

This time instead of going straight to my inbox, I went to a Google Doc and started making a game plan for myself (which I called my growth plan) based on what I had learned about mindset from Rick, about leadership from TT and about culture from Sandy.

I also took into consideration the conversation with Robert Coachman before driving home from Bella Medical, as well as what Amelia and I had talked about the last couple days.

In addition, I was determined to start growing from the motions instead of just going through the motions, and to plan out my work, then work out my plan.

First, I decided to work on my elite mindset skills: Be better at where my feet are, be present, and give complete focus and attention to the moment.

I dedicated myself to remembering tomorrow and flipping the mental switch on and off when arriving home, starting with a digital sunset this evening.

And I decided to focus on improving my connection with Amelia and Rhys, vowing to be home for dinner at least three nights a week and to implement the *no cell phone* policy at the table.

Also, I decided to elevate my character by moving from the Golden Rule to the Platinum Rule, away from the focus of treating others how I want to be treated and focusing instead on treating others how they wanted to be treated.

And I realized that it was time to start using the elite culture philosophy of saying what you see and trusting the intent, to be more courageous to have the tougher, yet open and honest conversations. I need to have these types of dialogues with my team members at Bella Medical and with my wife at home so that I can improve communication, create clarity and create a plan to get on the same page to work better together as a team.

I want to behave more out of principles than preference and live in alignment with my one-word brand of *intention*.

Also, I have decided to say *no* to all the meetings, events and other work-related commitments that I chose to participate in. Instead, I will empower my team members to make more decisions without my input. That will help me to be more present at home and will move Bella Medical to being team member *led*, rather than executive *fed*.

It's time to work on setting a misogi with my best friend and bride Amelia so we can bond closer together through having more time and shared adversity. Not quite sure what it will be, but maybe a rim-to-rim-to rim self-sustained trek at the Grand Canyon. I promised Amelia years ago that I would take her and we still haven't gone, even though she pushed me to do so for years. She finally lost hope and stopped pressing.

I looked at the sign on the wall in the pool house, *HOPE – Hold On, Possibilities Exist.* But this time, being more present, I noticed another sign beneath it: *HOPE – Hear Other People's Experiences.*

CHAPTER 48
Elite Results

That night at the dinner table, my first steps back into the home we had moved into four years ago, Amelia, Rhys and I sat, ate, laughed, talked, cried and enjoyed the love and presence of each other in the absence of our phones.

After dinner Rhys hugged me and said, "I'm so happy Daddy's back. I've missed you, Daddy. Can we do dinner again tomorrow night?"

As I hugged Rhys just a bit tighter and just a bit longer, Amelia and I made eye contact and we both shed a tear in that magical moment.

Over the coming days, weeks, months and years, the pandemic went away and so did the old Michael.

As the new Michael, I was equipped with the entire skillset pertaining to mindset, leadership, and culture. I also began to see record-setting results at the office and an amazing environment at home.

I was offered another promotion and decided that what I really wanted was a demotion in the office to free up time to accept a promotion at home. So, I went back to a position I'd once held at Bella where I was in charge of training and development of new team members, allowing me to spend more time developing people and less time in my inbox.

I also created more time at home and took Amelia on the misogi through the Grand Canyon. Although that turned out to be harder and longer than I expected, it was well worth it.

Most of all, I was finally at peace with myself. I was all in on the journey and with my new process-oriented mindset, I got to experience the journey in a more meaningful way every day. The new mindset allowed me to understand that the journey from here to there was far better than both here and there. I had taken my eyes off the prize, the end result, and fixated them on the next step in front of me.

As a result, I became a journeyman, a person who embraces and chooses to enjoy each step of the journey.

And I had learned that it's a choice to go on the journey of developing an elite mindset, elite leadership skills, and building an elite culture or environment around you.

It's a choice available to anyone. It's a choice and a journey that produces elite results.

QUESTIONS FOR REFLECTION

(#1) <u>CHAPTER #10</u>: Rick mentions *"be where your feet are"* – a concept that runs throughout the book.

What does it mean to you to be where your feet are? What pulls your focus and attention away from being where your feet are?

(#2) <u>CHAPTER #8</u>: Rick says, *"I'm focused on being where my feet are, getting my mind right and my game tight. I'm focused on winning the day, not agonizing about the past or stressing about the future, just stacking quality days on top of quality days. It's a mindset that I love to share because I love what that mindset has done for me, my business and my family."*

What's the stress about the future or the past that you hold on to? What are your strategies to let that go and better engage in the journey and the present moment?

(#3) <u>CHAPTER #9</u>: Rick says, *"I am a firm believer that our physiology affects our psychology and our psychology affects our physiology."*

What strategies do you implement in your life to positively affect your physiology and your psychology?

(#4) <u>**CHAPTER #10**</u>:   Rick says, *"Our focus determines our future, and awareness is the first step in all growth. What you are aware of you can alter; what you are unaware of will alter you."*

What do you do to better improve your skills of focus and awareness?

(#5) <u>CHAPTER #11</u>: What does the concept of "Remember Tomorrow" mean to you? How can that be beneficial in your life personally and professionally?

(#6) <u>CHAPTER #12</u>: Rick says, *"I like to think that there's no use worrying about the things you can control because if you can control them, why worry? There's also no use worrying about the things you can't control because if you can't control them, why worry?"*

Please make a list of what's in your control and what's outside of your control. Then reflect on what percentage of the time you are fixated on what you can't control versus what you can control. How can you make a shift in that focus as well as on the skill of process over outcome?

(#7) <u>CHAPTER #13</u>: What do you do to "flip the mental switch?" What's an example of this in your life?

(#8) <u>CHAPTERS #14–15</u>: Do you agree with the statement that "Decisions determine destiny"? What did you take from the story of the O'Hares that you can apply to your life?

(#9) <u>**CHAPTER #16**</u>: What are the most essential parts of your daily and weekly routines? What are your most critical success habits?

(#10) **CHAPTER #17**: What is your time management system? How do you stay organized and keep track of your time? What does your ideal day and ideal week look like? What gets in the way of you executing your ideal day and ideal week on a consistent basis?

(#11) <u>CHAPTER #18</u>: How do you use mental rehearsal in your life? What do you think about Rick's statement that *"We are the competition?"*

(#12) <u>CHAPTER #19</u>: Which of the four aspects of emotional intelligence would you say is your strongest and which needs the most work? Why?

- Self-awareness
- Self-management
- Social awareness
- Relationship management

(#13) <u>CHAPTER #21</u>: As you reflect on the best teams you have ever been a part of, what were the characteristics of those teams that made them so great?

(#14) <u>CHAPTER #23</u>: TT says, *"The problem is never the problem. How you handle the problem is always the problem. Since it's you that's handling the problem, you are part of the problem."*

What's your thought on that statement?

(#15) <u>CHAPTER #24</u>: What are the three steps of the ownership process and how do you move your team members along the journey into steps 1, 2 and 3?

(#16) <u>CHAPTER #25</u>: How important do you believe connection is to building trust and being an effective leader? What's one of your best strategies for building connection? What gets in the way of you building connection with the people you lead?

(#17) <u>CHAPTER #26</u>: How important do you believe character is to building trust and being an effective leader? What's one of your best strategies for building the skill of character?

What are the behaviors that will make others question your character and the behaviors that will erode your character skill as a leader?

(#18) <u>CHAPTER #27</u>: How important do you believe consistency is to building trust and being an effective leader? What's one of your best strategies for building the skill of consistency?

What are the behaviors that will make others believe you are consistent as a leader? What will make others question your consistency as a leader?

(#19) <u>CHAPTER #28</u>: How important do you believe communication is to building trust and being an effective leader? What's one of your best strategies for improving your communication skill and being an effective communicator as a leader?

What are the behaviors that will make others believe you are an effective communicator as a leader? What will make others question your communication skills as a leader?

(#20) <u>**CHAPTER #29**</u>**:** How important do you believe creating clarity is as it relates to building trust and being an effective leader? What's one of your best strategies for increasing clarity as a leader?

What are the behaviors that will make others believe you create clarity as a leader? What will make others question your ability to create clarity as a leader?

(#21) <u>CHAPTER #30</u>: How important do you believe competence is to building trust and being an effective leader? What's one of your best strategies for improving your competence as a leader?

What are the behaviors that will make others believe you are a competent leader? What will make others question your competence as a leader?

(#22) <u>CHAPTER #31</u>: How important do you believe commitment is to building trust and being an effective leader? What's one of your best strategies for displaying and improving your commitment as a leader?

What are the behaviors that will make others believe you are committed as a leader? What will make others question your commitment as a leader?

(#23) <u>CHAPTER #32</u>: How important do you believe courage is to building trust and being an effective leader? What is one of your best strategies for developing the skill of courage as a leader?

What are the behaviors that will make others believe you are courageous as a leader? What will make others question your courage as a leader?

(#24) <u>CHAPTER #37</u>: By definition, culture is a set of beliefs that drive our behaviors. How important do you believe an organization's culture is to the success of the organization?

What do you see as strategies to help build a positive and productive culture? What can destroy a culture and create a toxic environment?

(#25) <u>**CHAPTER #38:**</u>   What's your personal mission statement?   Why is your personal mission statement important to you?

Have you ever worked in an organization where they had a mission statement and it seemed that nobody in the organization knew what it was, what it stood for, or why it was created in the first place?

(#26) <u>**CHAPTER #39:**</u> What's a vision that you have in your life and that you have for this year and this quarter? Why is that vision important to you? What must you start, stop and continue to help you bring that vision into fruition?

(#27) <u>CHAPTER #40</u>: What are your personal core principles? What are the core principles of your organization? Why is it important that we have individual core principles and a collective shared set of core principles in our organization?

(#28) <u>**CHAPTER #41:**</u> What's your one-word brand? Why? What are you doing well? What do you want to do better, and how are you going to do it, as it relates to living your one-word brand?

R #42: What is your why? Please
times, as to WHY what you wrote
Go deep, dig deep. Why is your
hy? What's the deep underlying
ie your 7 layers of why.

(#30) <u>CHAPTER #43</u>: What are (or should be) at least five of your unyielding non-negotiables?

(#31) <u>CHAPTER</u> #44: What's a misogi that you have for this year? What about for your life? Why did you set these as misogi's for yourself? What's the benefit if you are able to achieve them?

(#32) <u>CHAPTER #45</u>:   What's the four-step success formula? Please list a specific behavior or action that you can take to implement each of the steps.

(#33) <u>CHAPTER #46</u>: Sandy tells Michael, *"If you don't use it, you will lose it."*

What are three strategies that you are going to implement in your life from reading this book? How specifically are you going to use those strategies?

ABOUT THE AUTHOR

 Todd Cetnar, MPM, is an author, speaker and accelerator. The founder and CEO of Cetnar Consulting Group, he has 25+ years leading strategic growth with prominent companies and sports teams across the globe.

He is a former professional basketball player and 3x Hall of Famer who played throughout Europe. Today he serves as a Vice President of Sales for a leading medical device company.

As a corporate executive, Todd combined the skill sets he learned in both business and athletics to formulate a results-delivering system called *The 3 Pillars of Elite Results.*

Todd travels globally to coach corporate executives, organizations, coaches, athletes and teams on the skills they need to develop the mindset, leadership and culture it takes to achieve elite results.

CONNECT WITH TODD

 @CetConsultGroup

 /CetnarConsulting

 /CetnarConsultingGroup

 /CetnarConsultingGroup

 @CetnarConsultingGroup

CONTACT TODD?

Contact Todd to inquire about having him come speak with you and your team, school or organization so you can start getting elite results!

Contact Todd by visiting
CetnarConsultingGroup.com/contact
TODD'S NEWSLETTER

Stay connected with Todd and get his strategies, system and results-driving content delivered straight to your inbox with his newsletter. Sign up for Todd's 'Elite Club' on his homepage to receive his newsletter.

To receive Todd's newsletter, visit CetnarConsultingGroup.com/newsletter

TODD'S PODCAST

Stay connected with Todd and get his strategies, system and results-driving content as you drive and participate in "automobile university" with Todd's *3 Pillars of Elite Results* podcast.

To listen to Todd's *3 Pillars of Elite Results* podcast, visit CetnarConsultingGroup.com/podcast

KEYNOTE SPEAKING

Todd delivers his message with energy and enthusiasm to help educate, empower and energize his audiences. If you are looking for a keynote speaker who will energize your team/staff and leave them with simple and powerful strategies to optimize their mindset, leadership and culture while accelerating results, contact Todd today.

**To inquire about booking Todd
to speak at your next event, visit
CetnarConsultingGroup.com/speaking**

1-on-1 COACHING

Todd works one-on-one with CEOs, executives, coaches and athletes on developing The 3 Pillars of Elite Results: The Mindset, Leadership and Culture You Need to Succeed in Business, Sports and Life.

Todd now offers 1-on-1 coaching opportunities where he works with you directly to apply the information in this book to your life, so that you can accelerate your results on the path to becoming your best self. This 1-on-1 Coaching is Todd's **most exclusive program** and there are a limited number of spots available.

**Get started today by visiting
CetnarConsultingGroup.com/coaching**

TEAM CONSULTING

Todd works with teams in the athletic and corporate arenas on developing The 3 Pillars of Elite Results: The Mindset, Leadership and Culture You Need to Succeed in Business, Sports and Life.

Todd offers the opportunity to work directly with your team so that you can apply the information in this book to your performance and accelerate your results.

**Get started today by visiting
CetnarConsultingGroup.com/consulting**

Made in the USA
Las Vegas, NV
28 July 2021

27187765R00095